Advance Praise

"Exploring the deep call of a Saami blood line, Riekki couples wonder, spirit, loss and anger in skilled poetry and gripping prose, all laced with *North*—the place where the water is—as a force of identity. His multi-genre collection will absorb readers with the power of both a totemic story and the deep lyricism of a lost people. He is perhaps a reindeer, and if you follow him into this book, you may, briefly and purely, enter their world."

> — Anne-Marie Oomen, author of *Love, Sex and 4-H* (Next Generation Indie Award for Memoir); *Uncoded Woman*, a collection of poetry; and co-author of *Lake Michigan Mermaid*

"In *My Ancestors Are Reindeer Herders And I Am Melting In Extinction,* Ron Riekki's Saami-American voice gives shape to the questions that haunt all of us. The book begins with a shriek and a howl and a warning about human-made dangers, including radiation, prison, war, metaphors, and suicide. He then teaches us to pay attention to things that can seep into our souls. He asks us to think about what we have allowed to become endangered and tangled. As he writes around themes of survival and identity, he recognizes the way language, love, and listening can be antidotes for the stress of needing to un-know what the world has become. In his poems and stories there is pain but also dancing beneath the blinking stars, across land we know is medicine, knowing not every hunger can be satisfied and somewhere there are still reindeer herders circling the arctic."

> — Margaret Noodin, author of *Weweni: Poems in Anishinaabemowin and English*

"With his latest collection of verse and prose, Ron Riekki depicts a compelling and powerful new vision of Sámi America, a hidden landscape of nonrecognition, intersectional identities, and Indigenous ways of being threatened by the modern world. Riekki's raw, confessional verse is reflective and fresh, like the stirring breath of thawing earth in the spring. Within this world of displaced Indigeneity, of culture fragmented and reconfigured, we are surrounded by ghosts—metaphorical and literal—that live alongside us in a poisoned world on the brink of collapse. Staring unwaveringly into the deep uncertainty of a present not of our own making, Riekki begins the arduous work of resisting extinction by building new futures from the fragments of the past, listening to the whispers of ghosts, carried to us beneath the chickadee's wing, on the back of the brisk winter wind."

— Dr. Tim Frandy, Assistant Professor of Folk Studies at Western Kentucky University

"To write with full knowledge of all sides of your being—not just sing with it, but cry out with it, and yes, yell with thousands of your ancestors when needed...Ron Riekki has done this. To fight daily for the existence of your people through the war on words, Riekki is in the thick of the Indigenous struggle. Loss of language, culture, pain of boarding schools...Indigenous is Indigenous."

— Sally Brunk, Keweenaw Bay Indian Community-Anishinaabe poet, writer, and storyteller, author of *The Cliffs: Summer Soundings*

MY ANCESTORS ARE REINDEER HERDERS AND I AM MELTING IN EXTINCTION

MY ANCESTORS ARE REINDEER HERDERS AND I AM MELTING IN EXTINCTION

Saami-American Non-Fiction, Fiction, and Poetry

Ron Riekki

Apprentice House Press
Loyola University Maryland

First Edition

Paperback ISBN: 978-1-62720-211-4
Ebook ISBN: 978-1-62720-212-1

Printed in the United States of America

Design by Gianna Walker
Edited by Gianna Walker
Promotion by Kelly Lyons

Published by Apprentice House Press

Apprentice House Press
Loyola University Maryland
4501 N. Charles Street
Baltimore, MD 21210
410.617.5265 • 410.617.2198 (fax)
www.ApprenticeHouse.com
info@ApprenticeHouse.com

dedicated to my parents, my grandparents, and Nils-Aslak Valkeapää

Giitu.

Contents

As Previously Published

Hotel Amerika—"You Dig"

The Airgonaut—"Čoavdda"

New Madrid—"Two"

S/tick: Feminists on Guard/Don't Die Press—"Love Note to Vuorwro"

Bird's Thumb—"Red"

The New Verse News—"My Grandmother, a Shaman, Has Words For Those Who Voted for Trump"

Alternating Current Press—"I'm Worried That I'm Not"

Duende—"The Images"

Clade Song—"Reindeer"

Canary: A Literary Journal of the Environmental Crisis—"Death and Taxonomies"

Rappahannock Review—"Pokoinikk"

Breadcrumbs Mag—"The People in the Bible"

Grub Street Literary Magazine—"Veahkki"

Rigorous: a journal edited and written by people of color—"For the People Who are Indigenous"

Rigorous: a journal edited and written by people of color—"This is the First Poem You Have Bled by Someone of Saami Descent"

Rigorous: a journal edited and written by people of color—"My Indigenous Roots Have Been Buried"

Rigorous: a journal edited and written by people of color—"I Am"

elsewhere—"I'm Sámi"

Expanded Horizons: Speculative Fiction for the Rest of Us—"Vuorwro"

elsewhere—"To the Seven Bars in Our Town of 4,614 People"

Virtual Artists Collective's All Roads Will Lead You Home—"The Rejection of the Upper Peninsula of Michigan"

Five:2:One—"My Indigenous Roots"

Soundings East—"I Grew Up in a Town So Cold That Even the Ice Could Not Commit Suicide"

Gloom Cupboard—"Indigenous"

Gloom Cupboard—"Saami-American"

Burningword Literary Journal—"Setting the Landlord on Fire"

Coldfront—"'Kiälláseh' by Amoc, featuring Ailu Valle"

Causeway Lit—"My Ancestors" (honorable mention for 2017 Poetry Contest)

Barking Sycamores: Neurodivergent literature and its craft—"Shaman / *Noaidi*"

Lycan Valley Press Publications—"The *Novealla* of Vuorwro (#6)"

Canary: A Literary Journal of the Environmental Crisis and *KYSO Flash: Knock-Your-Socks-Off Art and Literature*—"Collusion"

Dos Gatos Press—"On the Road in Colorado"

Dos Gatos Press—"I Am the Only Saami"

New Madrid—"i have been warned not to write about this (the erasure of moon so there is only sun)"

Canary: A Literary Journal of the Environmental Crisis—"My Girlfriend and Her Two Friends, A Mile Outside Yosemite"

Shot Glass Journal: Online Journal of Short Poetry—"Hiking with My Girlfriend"

The Journal of Sustainability Education: Decolonizing and Sustainability Education—"Saami (ruovttugiella)"

The Journal of Sustainability Education: Decolonizing and Sustainability Education—"The White Kid at the Native American Camp"

previously unpublished—"Same"

The Journal of Sustainability Education: Decolonizing and Sustainability Education—"Her-it-age"

Foreword

*I swore never to be silent whenever and wherever human beings
endure suffering and humiliation. We must always take sides.
Neutrality helps the oppressor, never the victim.
Silence encourages the tormentor, never the tormented.*

*—Elie Wiesel, Acceptance Speech on the occasion of the award of the
Nobel Peace Prize in Oslo, December 10, 1986*

I read poetry every day. I read poetry the way I imagine some read Bible verse, others the stock market report. I read poetry because I'm pulled, like a tragedy, into the wisdom of a poem. Once, on a plane to Florida a four-year-old named Aly sat in the window seat in front of me. When she poked her head around to talk to me, I asked her why she loves flying. She said that she loves "bouncing on the clouds" and seeing the cars – the way they look like "moving candy." I read poetry because I need *bouncing on the cloud* moments every day. I need engagement of intelligence and imagination. I want images to be portraits of things that speak beyond the image itself – something I can enter into metaphorically, that heightens or intensifies understanding, something that gives a deeper knowing.

In the last several decades there has been a proliferation of writers and writing programs. The country has gone a bit book-club crazy too. Perhaps technology and its rapid effects on social changes, its cold muscularity and formality has created a craving in us. We need, through literature, to be reminded of the pulse of light in the belly of fireflies. And the way grief is its own book of knowledge, a diary of sorts. Literature reminds us that we are painfully, ecstatically human. To experience something of another human being's life, to see life from their perspective, to the extent that we can, is not only fascinating, but tantalizes us into testing ourselves emotionally. The personal *is* the universal. Besides, it is our duty to pay attention to ourselves and the planet. Not to be heard, or worse, to be treated with indifference, is to become spiritually extinct.

Images, music, stories are sacred things. Even the story of where you bought your new shoes can contain spiritual underpinnings. It may be that the telling itself, *how* it is told, allows us to connect with one another. When we experience a lyrical quality, we begin to understand ourselves in the *once-upon-a-times* of story-telling and we begin to see that The Sacred exists everywhere, in everything—in our daily trips to Costco; in the hands of the checkout woman; in the bones of our ancestors resting peacefully at the edge of the river. This is the knowing that Ron Riekki gives us again and again in *My Ancestors are Reindeer Herders and I am Melting in Extinction.*

"America died on Nov. 8, 2016," Bill Moyers tells us, "not with a bang or a whimper, but at its own hand via electoral suicide. We the people chose a man who has shredded our values, our morals, our compassion, our tolerance, our decency, our sense of common purpose, our very identity—all the things that, however tenuously, made a nation out of a country." Against this unbearable backdrop, we need voices like Riekki's to remove the filters that keep us from feeling. The world that Riekki shows us is a world of disenfranchisement and genocide, a world where indigenous people like the Saami of northern Europe, Riekki's people, have been forcibly erased and artificially assimilated. As an insider/outsider, Riekki sees American "values" for what they are and throws clean punches at so-called moral choices. "I have looked around in those darkened theaters and been horrified at the people inside, what they find funny," he writes.

What I love about *My Ancestors are Reindeer Herders and I am Melting in Extinction* is the way Riekki grapples with identity and explodes injustice, resisting a system that would reduce everybody to a worker and everything to a commodity. "The reindeer," he reminds us, "were the heart of our religious symbolism/up until the time they turned us into witches." Although Riekki comes from an aboriginal people who have lost their language through linguicide and erasure (not to mention genocide), he nevertheless powerfully gives voice to his ancestors. Where a best friend talks to his dead father's ghost (who has no mouth), Riekki speaks for him. Where oral tradition was silenced by the loss of the Saami language, Riekki's ancestors return ghost-like to open their mouths, to offer us sermons, to allow us to float with them on the river and listen to the loon. We are asked to contemplate our own suicide, and choose life for the sake of another. Riekki's language has the power to transform, to make us feel alive and less alone in the world; it offers a collective understanding.

Riekki's memoirs, stories, and poems also whisper the word *empathy* and at times, make me laugh, in a luscious Lenny Bruce kind of way. Perhaps this is Riekki's most personal book, where memoir is confessional, fiction revelatory, and poetry an immediacy of powerful feelings. In *My Ancestors are Reindeer Herders and I am Melting in Extinction* the dead become our storytellers, prisons our collective consciousness, the rivers of Michigan our solace. We too, on the back of a Harley, feel barely able to hang on. Yet we do, because just when we're about to fall off we're reminded of the bear and "its body as wide as the stars" crossing the road in front of us "like a monk." Bear as homily, its life offered as courage, strength, as having a *right* to exist. Bear, as undisputable, as alleviation from fake news.

The Holocaust attempted to erase my people. My mother-in-law survived where nine siblings and her parents did not, murdered by government policy. I feel duty bond to make proclamations on their behalf. "Everywhere we went the trains came with us," I write in my poem "Children of Survivors." This is one of the jobs of the poet/writer. To proclaim truth, tell your ghost stories, not to be silent against injustice. "I have bear ritual in my veins" Riekki writes. "I need aurora borealis to live… /while I struggle for food in this post-Obama mood where/ the leaders haven't stepped inside of schools, let alone/ inside pow wows…"

If, as poet Andrea Hollander Budy tells us, poetry is "the human voice singing the hidden side of things," Riekki's book is a *Hamilton*—rebellious, historical, necessary—a full-on musical.

—*Joy Gaines-Friedler, Winner of the 2016 Poetry Society of Michigan Margo Lagattuta Poetry Prize*

You Dig

for Olavi Paltto

When we found out they were down
by the river digging up our indigenous
all, we shoplifted quicker legs to run

down to the woods where we could
watch them fuck up graveyards meant
to be treated like flowers, gentle, sacred,

but we decided to wait for the sun to go
drown in the nearby lake where we'd
emerge with our shadows tucked under

our arms and, casket-eyed, howling all-
kill oaths at the top of our throats so
that they'd run in the only other direction—

into the river—where they'd struggle in
the night, when we've had to struggle
for ten million days straight and our

ancestors would join in the shrieking,

warning the anthropologists or grave-
robbers or whatever they nightmared

in their minds that they were, or are,
their museum-minds with prison-bar
thoughts, and we'd re-own the wind.

Čoavdda

I am looking for a key in a Utah hazmat field.

The deer look for leaves in the same field. They look for radioactive leaves. They don't know that the leaves are radioactive. I don't know that there's no key. This is called hazing. This is called being a rookie. A pawn. The nighttime is cold but they have only issued me a short-sleeve shirt. I am hazmat security. I make sure no one tries to steal plutonium or uranium or other things that will melt their skin.

We do not fear terrorists, to be honest with you; we fear bored teenagers. We fear bored teenagers who think NO TRESPASSING signs are solely for Christians, who think DANGER signs are welcome mats.

We have had six arrests since I've been here—all of them white teenage bored slightly drunk slightly buzzed slightly stupid kids. My coworker says the deer are the same—stupid; he says we should kill all of the deer on site. The deer all have polyneuropathy. The deer look caught in headlights even when it is pitch dark. They stumble and stare into space and could be extras in zoological zombie movies. The site where I work, I am told, does animal testing and does nuclear experimentation and houses aliens and is one of the leading centers for oncological advancement in the world. The site seems to do everything, but my boss says to me, "Look, all we do is store hazmat material." I think of that term, what he is saying: *hazardous materials material*. Even the signs here are redundant: DANGER DO NOT ENTER DANGER and a run-on sign saying BIOHAZARD AREA HAZMAT AREA RESTRICTED

AREA. They repeat words like 'Danger' and 'Area' as if sheer repetition is all that is needed for warning. The police, by the way, rarely come here. They are wise. I had to sign a waiver saying that I am OK with X amount of radiation per year. That was six years ago. I have X times 6 amount of radiation at this point.

We have no employees who have worked here longer than nine years. The reason, I am told, is that they don't want to give raises. A coworker tells me it's because the radiation exposure is too high after a decade. Another coworker says that after nine years they worry you'll find out the truth about the aliens stored in the center hub building. There are no aliens, because aliens do not exist. Hazmat does exist. Deer who can't walk correctly anymore exist. I look at the deer. I am Sámi, an indigenous people of the Arctic. My ancestors were reindeer herders. They came to the U.S. to escape Russian and Nazi invasion, to avoid the forced sterilizations of Sweden.

My girlfriend is worried I won't be able to have children because of this job. I tell her I am lucky to have a job. I tell her I am blessed to have a job. She tells me I sound like an evangelical, like a gambler, like someone brainwashed. She tells me I should get a job as security in a bank. I tell her there is no possibility I can get shot guarding hazmat. On average, I see about two people per night. I see the person I relieve and I see the person who relieves me. The night, every night, is so desperately haunted with nothing that I am free to forget my life. I look up at the stars and think of the hydrogen in their cores, their cosmological radioactive guts, their electromagnetic astronomical stomachs.

I have a growth in my intestines. The doctor tells me not to worry about it. I have pretty good health insurance. He says if it gets too large, they will take it out. He says if it were a hundred years ago I would have something to worry about. A hundred years ago I wouldn't know I have a growth in my intestines; I'd be beautifully oblivious. I look at the deer and speak to it, asking if it knows that my ancestors would have worshipped it. I tell the deer my grandfather moved to the U.S. because he wanted to give us a new life. I wonder if my grandfather would have understood hazmat, the way his grandson would search on hands and knees in a field on his seventh day on the job, a field clearly marked with DO NOT ENTER signs. I think of gastroenterology, the doctor I have been going to. Énteron is Ancient Greek for 'intestines.' He tells me the radiation probably entered me from all the times I've eaten at work, all the times I didn't wash my hands and I swallowed the unthinkable. He says he doesn't know for sure, that it might have happened in a thousand other ways as well. He says anything can happen.

Deer are painted on the sacred drums, have their images woven into holy blankets.

The deer here chews, a leaf on its chin, its eyes frighteningly cute.

My assimilated father used to tell me that God would seep into you. He said that Jesus is like an infection. For some reason, for him it was always disease metaphors with Christ. Nuns would hit my grandfather if he ever spoke Finn. He'd get beat brutally with rulers if he ever mentioned Sápmi.

All of the Sámi languages are critically endangered. We use the same wording with language that we do with the extinction of animals.

I look up. My ancestors believed the stars were the hoof prints of the great reindeer that ran across the sky. I look at the field where I crawled as a newly employed baby. The deer walks in the same path where my body went. I wonder if I am the deer.

Two

When I played college basketball,
six of us from the team slept in a garage
with no heat, no hot water, cheap rent, no lock

on the door so that my shirts were stolen
and a helicopter one night flashed
a spotlight down on me while I peed

on a bush; I shook, flipping off
the pilot. My best friend was a Te-Moak
Tribe point guard, a Shoshone named

Jose who told me he was the same
height and skin color as a fire hydrant.
I never told him I'm Saami because

we spent too much time laughing
in the cold on the three-point-line concrete
in a forgotten Vallejo park with sick

angels resting in the sky. We threw
rocks at the stars and he pretended
the reservation was a dream and I

remember pow wows as a kid where
I felt like one-half, the thrill of smoke,
a river in my hometown where I'd

walk down its center for hours
before the mines turned it orange,
and I realize now, my thyroid

gathering flames, that midnight
free throws held more peace
than seven thousand prayers.

Love Note to Vuorwro

My mother would wander into my room
at night with ghost stories. She was filled
with haunting. I'd be thirsty for her horror.

With just moonlight, she'd tell me Sámi
tales, saying our tradition was oral, meaning
you just needed ears and tongues, that words

are bodily, and in her tales girls and boys
would be ripped apart in the end. She'd turn
off a light that was already off and creak up

the punished stairs. Her favorite: Vuorwro,
a spirit who would wander the night, entering
rooms where there was no water. She'd eat

everyone in the room, turning throats to straws
where she would suck down stomachs and
leave just specks of gnawed bones behind.

My mother told me that Vuorwro was a hero,
that the worst thing to do was to stay in one
place forever, that we were born nomads

and we had to search for the blood that would
keep us alive. I asked her if she meant that
I should kill people too. And she said, *Vuoi!*

Of course not. She said that it was metaphor
and I asked what metaphor was and she threw
open her mouth and swallowed my spine.

Red

Disenfranchisement has become a franchise.

Franchise comes from Old French and Middle English for 'free.' You'll notice that this word for 'freedom' comes from colonial languages. We aren't told the etymological link to Algonquin, because it's an extinct language, a slaughtered language, a tongue-eviscerated language.

In English, the word *sacred* is a part of *massacred*, as if the language itself hints at the justifying of kills. And both end with *red*, the skin that has been in this liminal state between is aboriginal sacred roots and its colonial unoriginal genocidal ripping up of roots. But when the violence gets out of control (see the long, long list of school shootings), then we start saying we need to do something. We never do anything.

It isn't common knowledge that *mænno* and *friija* and *friddja* are Saami words for 'free,' because all of the current Saami languages are on the UNESCO endangered languages list. I wish we cared about the Nenets in Russia or Maori in Australia the way we care about the extinction of the hawksbill turtle or Ganges River dolphin.

I used to work in a prison, at a nursing station. I volunteered at another prison, teaching writing. When I taught writing, I found that the prisoners were just as intelligent as the students at the nearby university in Alabama. When I was at Brandeis, I cross-registered at Radcliffe. I found that the Alabama students were just as intelligent as Harvard students. Honestly, there's no intellectual difference between a Harvard student and a prisoner. The difference is opportunity. I could do a racist-classist-sexist-homophobic hegemonic hermeneutics academic sentence here, but that language is becoming cliché in the way that I've gone to church services and heard the entire Colonial-Christ language recited by what sounded like old robots. In contrast, I visited a transsexual-transvestite church in San Francisco and my girlfriend said it was the most alive church she'd ever been to because the clichés were gone, replaced with true movement and passion for community, the beauty of transvestite hallelujahs. I sometimes think academic writing needs to be set on fire and replaced with reality; I'd enjoy watching the flames dance, their salsa of orange-red.

One of the surprising things about prison is how little movement there is. The cells where I worked were solitary confinement. You could stretch your hands out and reach both sides. It was a place of madness. It seemed made to instill claustrophobia. *Claustrum-* comes from 'lock.' And the place seemed bathed in *phobia*. The fear of the lock. Xan, a girl in my improv class, said that her deepest fear is the inability to move freely. My girlfriend says she should be able to walk at night without every moment feeling like the deepest insides of a real haunted house.

Prison is taphophobia incarnate. It's being buried alive. Re: Poe.

Prison is *not* at all a place for rehabilitation. It's a place where you fake rehabilitation. Where prisoners are rewarded for counterfeiting what supposedly resembles rehabilitation. I had some homophobic, Islamophobic students in the south who were pro-incarceration, avid fans of prison sentences, wishing those prison sentences would turn into prison paragraphs, lives turned into prison novels. I've read that prisons are exponential generators of Islamic conversion, creators of sexual fluidity, that the things those Alabama students fear are what is being generated daily. I know gay Muslims; there is nothing to fear there. Much more deeply, I fear the homophobic Islamophobe with their gun fetish posts.

A friend of mine was incarcerated, twice. He said jail is community college, prison as university. It's where you go to network, to bond with other drug dealers and learn how to deal drugs better. Robbers discuss robbery with robbers, gaining tips on how not to get caught the next time. And there is a next time. The U.S. recidivism rates are self-created, with three-quarters of released prisoners rearrested within five years. Prison creates prison. Felonies lead to more felonies. The entire prison system needs CPR. It's begging for an AED. The very thing we think protects us is killing us. [See: guns.] Although it's all making private-prison Geo Group CEO George Zoley a multi-millionaire. (Geo Group is a *yuuuuuge* Trump supporter.)

I'm losing my place. That's what happens, I suppose. It's a fitting metaphor. I've been reading a lot of Sherman Alexie lately, listening to Native American comedy. It seems like it's a comedy about land, books about land, about lack of land. The word land comes from the German word *Land*. Das Land. In French, it's *terre*. Similar to *terreur*. I've been listening to a lot of Muslim comedy as well. Dave Chappelle, Azhar Usman, and Aasif Mandvi all do an incredible job at attacking the terror that is Trump.

Terror and territory and Trump.

My father told me I'm Saami. Native European. He said his grandparents were Laplanders, reindeer herders. I tried to find out if that's true genealogically, but his parents have the brutal stories/histories of the indigenous, the gaps and slippage and absence. Alcohol is its own genocide. He said it's true familially, as part of our handed-down ancestral narrative, our story.

The dead don't speak. No, that's not true. They yell to us, daily.

Reading is like trying to hold a wet fish.

History is like trying to hold a ghost.

I am worried I'm going extinct, that the easy way I can be dismissed as simply white is a way of ensuring the Saami in me will die. There is a massive conservative eraser, one that keeps scrubbing hard at the earth, at the heart, with its theater of politics, the heater of de-regulation. We went from the hope of change of Obama to the hole of climate change of Trump. Extinction happens one animal at a time, one person at a time, one identity at a time, one language at a time, one day at a time, one four-year period at a time.

Sweden attempted to make the Saami extinct through decades of compulsory sterilizations that no one seems to ever talk about. Decades of forced sterilization. Decades.

In Swedish, the word for genocide is *folkmord*.

I tried to take a Scandinavian folklore class at Berkeley. The teacher said it was filled, adding that I wasn't Scandinavian. He said Finland had nothing to do with Scandinavian folklore. He asked what I'd even want to write about for the class. I was interested in the *Kalevala*, Finland's national epic that's a mesh of Finn and Karelian and Saami identity, the only book of my youth that I was told comes from the very sinus node of where I'm from, the center of the heart of my roots—Karjala and Taipalsaari and Kuusamo and more. My ancestors are eastern and northern Finns, areas that are markedly Euro-aboriginal, the same *Kalevala*-like Karelian/Saami interweaving. He replied I could write about how the *Kalevala* was stolen from Sweden. What? I remembered my speechlessness. This, mind you, was Berkeley, the land of supposed extreme liberalism, but with hypocritical vulgarly high rent prices and high ticket prices and high tuition prices and high gas prices and homeless-creating prices with everything. I wanted so badly to tell the instructor that the Saami were the *original* Scandinavians. But I kept silent. I still regret that.

When we speak of the indigenous, we're speaking of extinction, a word tied to the late Middle English for 'quench.' To satisfy one's thirst. To drink. Think Vlad the Impaler, the nut-case alive at the same time as Chris Columbus. Maybe they were the same person?

In Saami, the word north doesn't mean the same as the colonial 'north'. In Saami, the word north means 'to the coast.' Where the water is.

I only know one Saami dance and it resembles canoeists searching for land. It is a dance that reminds me of diaspora, of displacement. I showed the dance to my Performativity class and started crying. I realized the people in my class might never meet another Saami-connected person in their entire lives. I am saola. I am pangolin.

I grew up not far from the border of the U.S. and Canada. I speak English and French. My Finnish is horrible, my Saami worse. I recently went to a Finnish church and was shocked that I understood quite a bit from the pastor. My ancestors grew up near the border of Russia and Finland. The border shifted, repeatedly, through war. I am a liminal body with liminal arteries and liminal thoughts. We've lived balancing on borderlines. I used to like to walk railroad tracks as a child, balancing for miles. Disequilibrium feels like home.

There is Russia's genocide of the Karelians I could tell you about, but there isn't time anymore.

I'm worried that there isn't history anymore.

I'm worried there isn't time or history at this point, that both have been taken.

I have never heard of Old Algonquin or Middle Saami.

The Saami were put in human zoos for display. Archaeologist Cathrine Baglo, a Ph.D. student in Norway who writes about this, has said that the Sami liked to stay in zoos. A friend of mine said she'd like to see Cathrine Baglo in a zoo. When I walk down the street, people stop and stare at me. Some point at me. I have a body on display at all times. If you look different, you are treated as zoo animal, in grocery stores, in hospitals, in libraries, insane.

My mother complained to the city of Marquette about the zoo they had on Presque Isle. Its animals looked suicidal. They seemed to say in their eyes that God had been taken from them, replaced by the Devil of metal. Years later, the zoo was deconstructed. My mother was proud of that.

One day one of the prisoners shattered his cell's shatterproof glass. He picked up a shard as long as his arm, swinging it back and forth. The nurses ran from the upstairs nursing station to the downstairs station. They slammed the door bolted shut and sat by me. They told me the top floor was taken hostage. We waited. I asked if the glass to our nursing station was shatterproof.

One of the most stupid ideas in the history of America is Trump's wall. I think his dream is to have a Trump ceiling and three other Trump walls and then the entirety of America will become a Trump Tower. It will be a prison.

We all will be reading this for decades:

WALL WALL WALL WALL WALL WALL WALL WALL WALL
WALL WALL WALL WALL WALL WALL WALL WALL WALL WALL
WALL WALL WALL WALL WALL WALL WALL WALL WALL WALL
WALL WALL WALL WALL WALL WALL WALL WALL WALL WALL
WALL WALL WALL WALL WALL WALL WALL WALL WALL WALL
WALL WALL WALL WALL WALL WALL WALL WALL WALL WALL
WALL WALL WALL WALL WALL WALL WALL WALL WALL WALL
WALL WALL WALL WALL WALL WALL WALL WALL WALL WALL
WALL WALL WALL WALL WALL WALL WALL WALL WALL WALL
WALL WALL WALL WALL WALL WALL WALL WALL WALL WALL
WALL WALL WALL WALL WALL WALL WALL WALL WALL WALL
WALL WALL WALL WALL WALL WALL WALL WALL WALL WALL
WALL WALL WALL WALL WALL WALL WALL WALL WALL WALL
WALL WALL WALL WALL WALL WALL WALL WALL WALL WALL
WALL WALL WALL WALL WALL WALL WALL WALL WALL WALL
WALL WALL WALL WALL WALL WALL WALL WALL WALL WALL
WALL WALL WALL WALL WALL WALL WALL WALL WALL WALL
WALL WALL WALL WALL WALL WALL WALL WALL WALL WALL
WALL WALL WALL WALL WALL WALL WALL WALL WALL WALL
WALL WALL WALL WALL WALL WALL WALL WALL WALL WALL
WALL WALL WALL WALL WALL WALL WALL WALL WALL WALL
WALL WALL WALL WALL WALL WALL WALL WALL WALL WALL
WALL WALL WALL WALL WALL WALL WALL WALL WALL WALL
WALL WALL WALL WALL WALL WALL WALL WALL WALL WALL
WALL WALL WALL WALL WALL WALL WALL WALL WALL WALL
WALL WALL WALL WALL WALL WALL WALL WALL WALL WALL
WALL WALL WALL WALL WALL WALL WALL WALL WALL WALL
WALL WALL WALL WALL WALL WALL WALL WALL WALL WALL
WALL WALL WALL WALL WALL WALL WALL WALL WALL WALL
WALL WALL WALL WALL WALL WALL WALL WALL WALL WALL
WALL WALL WALL WALL WALL WALL WALL WALL WALL WALL
WALL WALL WALL WALL WALL WALL

one

day

we

will

tear
it
all
d
o
w
n
.

My Grandmother, a Shaman, Has Words For Those Who Voted for Trump

She recites a prayer, or perhaps it's a curse,
that the souls of the unjust will also have years
to howl, that their revelation will shake their heart

until their cobweb racism awakens the spiders
of their hate and they're forced to eat the insides
of their insides. She holds in her hand an iron pipe,

invisible, but visible, iron and air, and she sucks
deep on its end, telling me that she is taking away
their stupidity, gullibility, hegemonic ability,

and leaving them on vacation, meaning, etymologically
empty, vacated, so that something other than dumb
sexism can rest in their hollow bones. Her eyes

are fuses. Her skin reels. Her tears are middle

passages, saying we could have made history
but instead we made a bed to fuck the poor.

Behind her, there is no snow. We have assimilated
out of the Arctic, lost our language, bathed
in a drumless Michigan that has turned blood red

from apathy, tricked, pathetic, pricked to death
and not even realizing the rigor mortis. I watch
my mother open her mouth so wide that her lungs

are visible, iron and air, and I wonder if those
so easily swayed, so cinematographically fooled,
would even witness the protests of her body.

I'm Worried that I'm Not

indigenous enough, that I'm not
paying enough respect to my ancestors

and Arne says that worrying itself
is a disrespect to the ancestors,

that there should be no *paying*
as if the world is about money.

When he grew up, in his village,
there was no money. Northern

Canada. He says the first time
he saw money, he laughed at it.

He said that dollar bills are designed
in insane asylums and that they lack

the simplicity of rivers. He tells me
I am indigenous when I am with him

and we are out on the lake. He said
there is nothing to worry about

when we are peaceful with the earth,
with our heart, with our *váibmu*.

The Images

This piece of writing will alternate between non-fiction and fiction every paragraph. You may be thinking this paragraph must be non-fiction then, but everything is more complicated than that.

I have PTSD. I am getting tested to see if I have PTSD. Both my vet counselor and my social worker have already told me, "You have PTSD." They are seeing if it's service-related or just life-related, if the outside of the service unwrapped me as much as the inside of the service.

This week, for one of the extremely rare times in my life, I told another poet about my biggest terror. She asked me this while we were writing a collaborative poem. I asked her biggest fear and she told me, no, she couldn't talk about that. I asked her where it happened and she said in the Bay Area. She never told me what it was. She asked for my terror and I thought how my counselor said I need to start talking about this and took a deep breath and told her I wouldn't talk about it any more with her and that I would only tell her if she agreed to that and she shook her head yes and I said, "A helicopter on fire." She gasped or not gasped but gave a response like a gasp, more subtle, more excited, and then she wrote the thoughts that it triggered in her mind and I sat quietly and took a drink of bourbon.

I've had panic attacks. The first one I had was such an anaphylaxis of the soul that I can't even type it now or I'm worried I'll trigger another. I can't give you the details but it's the only moment I ever understood the psychology of zombies, the madness of the once-person running in those films. The error is thinking zombies are running *to* something. All of them are running away. Frantically.

I should've been rich. That cures everything. You can buy a Presidency if you're rich. The world is upside-down right now. We pretend it's not. America is fear.

I'm an empty stadium.

I'm not sure if I can tell you about the helicopter...

I can't. What it triggers in my body is an explosion of adrenaline, like I'm instantly inside Armageddon...

My old counselor told me to imagine a flower. He said to take the flames and turn them into the red of a rose. He said I had the power to do that. He insisted I have the power to do that. He said to take the red and to control it, to imagine with all of my might the most beautiful red flower I've ever seen and then see myself with that flower, the scent, its licorice-flavored leaves, the swallowtail butterfly feel of the petals. I got good at it. If I turned the light off at night to go to bed, the fire would come in my closed eyes and I'd turn the light back on immediately and look into the blinding brightness of the room and I'd force roses upon roses to be in front of my eyes and the melting humans inside would no longer melt and I'm tearful writing this and wondering why I am writing this, but I am writing this, perhaps because my counselor said I need to start getting it out, controlling it. I have written about this before but badly where I get lost in the way that I do not feel safe in history, which I think Robert Frost said or maybe Dan Chiasson talking about Robert Frost.

I'm cold. Arctic.

I found out recently that I'm Saami. I'm indigenous. European indigenous, which people don't know how to talk about. I've mentioned this in class and it's usually met with silence. There are estimated to be less than 100,000 Saami in the world. That's smaller than the population of the city where I live now.

I knew all along I was from Lapland, but I never understood the significance. I'm also Karelian. Indigenous Karelian, which again people don't know about. I've mentioned to people I'm Karelian and none of them have ever heard the word before. Except for two Russians I spoke with. One said, "It's beautiful there." I asked him to describe it but he said that he couldn't. He said there were woods and hills but I asked for more but he didn't have the words.

Linguicide. It's a word I learned while reading about Saami culture. I'm Kainuu Saami. Kainuu Saami language is dead.

I also found out I'm Middle Eastern. This is what ancestry.com does. It makes you realize you're not Belgian. At all. Even though that was the passed-down family history. Or it makes *me* realize I'm not Belgian. It resets your clock. It makes me think how much I want to know about what has been deleted. I see erasers of colonizers attacking the art of my ancestors. We are not what we think we are. You are not who you think you are. I promise.

Panic attacks. Listen to those harsh consonants. It's being cracked. I have emergency Temazepam in the other room. It's in case I need to be knocked out for the night, so that I can survive through sleep.

I have so much violence to tell you about. I'm glad there's a 2,500-word limit given by the editors to this journal. Otherwise I'd write a book.

In my Islam in the Public Sphere class that ends next week, Ibraham—the 60-year-old Muslim seriously genius law-school dropout student in the class—paraphrased a Ta-Nehisi Coates quote that 'to be black in America is to experience violence.'

I started thinking about how to be female in America is to experience violence.

And to be poor in America is to experience violence.

To be indigenous in America is to experience violence.

A group of boys, when I was riding my bike to go play Little League on the other side of my hometown of Negaunee, shattered my collarbone. I was in a brace for six months. I knew none of them. The wind was behind my back and I remember how happy that made me—and that's not an embellishment but the truth—and I was going downhill full speed when one of the boys kicked my front tire, a direct perfectly aimed blow, violent for no purpose. I went over the handlebars and cracked my collarbone, my body in a strange V so that I could see my shoulder in front of me, visible, grotesque. I remember the laughter from the other boys. It was the laughter I've heard during horror films, from those who enjoy when the woman is murdered with an ax; I have looked around in those darkened theaters and been horrified at the people inside, what they find funny.

I don't know why, but a wave of anger rushed through me just now.

I saw a movie once about a man who used to scream out of nowhere in his apartment; throughout the movie you find out the violence of his past and you understand why he screams. I forget the title. I forget every title. I just remember the images.

My counselor calls it 'intrusions.' It's when you can't get a horrific scene out of your mind, a photograph of hell.

I do not have 'flashbacks.' That's when you are caught in the past, caught in a movie of hell, everything moving, the film played on the blanket of the mind.

There was a horror film when I was a kid—I think it was called *Island of Terror*—about giant ugly turtle monsters that hid in trees and fell on you, crushing you, if you walked underneath. That scared the hell out of me.

I looked through binoculars that a Marine handed to me. At the helicopter.

A wave of anger was taking me over so I looked up some generic Halloween jokes to take my mind away:

What happened to the pirate ship that sank in the ocean?
It came back with a skeleton crew.
How did the skeleton know it was going to rain?
He could feel it in his bones.
How did the skeleton know it was raining?
He could feel it in his bones.
What do you call a skeleton that does stunts?
Bonehead.

It's what the company commander used to call us in boot camp. Bonehead.

Why the strange repetition of the same joke twice? It makes me think of the loops of time travel, the way we get stuck in the past, repeating, repeating, repeating.

In boot camp, we had a day where we had to stencil our uniforms. I was lucky I have a short name—Riekki. (It's a name that I was told means nothing. Then later I learned that it's Saami for 'ring': *riekkis*.) A kid named Maliwicki was stenciling nearby. His stencil wasn't working. Nothing works in the military. This was the Navy. He was behind. And the company commander was standing on the table while we did stenciling. Imagine someone standing on your table while you eat; it felt that strange. His feet would move by our heads. The C.C. barked at Maliwicki to speed up. Maliwicki said, "Sorry," which is stupid because you should always keep your mouth shut in the military. The problem was that you have to say "sir" at the end of everything. You're supposed to say, "I am bleeding, sir," "I am dying, sir," "I am dead, sir." Whatever the hell you wanted to speak, it had to end with that word. Maliwicki forgot. The C.C. said, "What did you just say?" And Maliwicki repeated, "'Sorry.'" Maliwicki sounded annoyed. We had only been there for days, some of them anyway. I got there early and had to wait for the rest of our company to arrive. It was purgatory until everyone got there, from everywhere in the U.S., every state, every background. Just nobody rich. The C.C. jumped down off the table so that he'd be right next to Maliwicki, hovering, and he said, "Say that again." Maliwicki said, "What?" and the C.C. punched him, hard. Maliwicki went down. I'm not sure if he punched Maliwicki in the face or the shoulder, but it looked like both. Everyone turned to look and quickly turned back to start stenciling again. It turned into Santa's workshop when the elves knew they were behind on schedule, the intensity magnified like prisons for dying men. We discovered we were professional pieces of rot.

The Company Commander never punched anyone again after that. He only had to do it once. We all knew it was waiting there, possible. It made everything official after that, frantic. Just making proper corners for your bunk would put you into fight-or-flight.

We had a kid from Texas punch a wall, breaking his hand, so they sent him home, 'medical discharge.'

My PTSD counselor said he makes it so we can see the sole door to his office at all times, the way the chairs are positioned. He said a lot of vets don't like to sit with their back to a door.

I worked in prison. I volunteered to teach English for a semester. Later I worked for a couple months as an EMT until I got attacked by one of the inmates. He threw liquid in my face. I wasn't sure if it was blood or piss or pus or water or spit or a combination. He threw two cups at me. The inmates weren't supposed to have cups at all, especially not two. Later, they told me they checked the inmate's charts and he didn't have HIV or hepatitis, but he could've gotten it since the last time he was tested. They said if I stayed, they were going to kill me. I'd tell you prison stories, but I get tired. Sometimes violence exhausts you.

In my Islam in the Public Sphere class, my professor talks about the hate emails and death threats that teachers of Islam receive. He told me he had a friend and a mentor both killed by ISIS. He said Islamophobes don't realize ISIS kills more Muslims than non-Muslims. He told me this after I mentioned how they had a cartoon of Saddam Hussein being raped on the wall where I worked in the Navy. It was sexually violent anti-Muslim caricatures on the wall. I complained and so they put me on the wall with racist, sexist, perverted comments directed at me. Art has the power to transform lives, to transform positively and hellishly, depending on the God or the Satan inside the person who does the art.

The helicopter is fading in my mind. It seems farther away each time I see it.

There was fog.

It flew into one of those mammoth crucifixes of electricity you see everywhere. It hung there. I hung there, looking at it. I shouldn't have looked. I looked. I'd tell you more but I'm running out of time. In this writing, in my life, in my writing life. Fifty is approaching and I'm looking for adjunct jobs with student debt enough to drown me forever. My girlfriend's brother committed suicide two years ago, cutting off his hand and bleeding to death in his backyard. I can't commit suicide and have her go through that again.

I'm Saami. I'm from a critically endangered people. I can't commit suicide when there are so few Saami left. I want to do the opposite of suicide. I want to connect with these groups from which I am both a part and apart. I've never met a person who's Saami other than relatives. If you're Saami, please write to me.

I struggle.

I remember reading from Nils-Aslak Valkeapää's *Eanni, Eannážan* who, on page 78, writes:

>   sin guovlu
>   SIN
>
>
>   SIN
>   eallin
>
>
>   SIN

I translate as:

>   their region
>   THEIRS
>
>
>   THEIR
>   life
>
>
>   THEIRS

I think of the two Americas we have now. The white-privilege male-privilege Christian-privilege hetero-privilege privilege-privilege of Trump and the multiracial, gender-bending, interreligious, fluid diversity of the rest of America.

When I did fundraising for gay marriage in L.A., a man in a pickup, his girlfriend passenger side, told me if he came back and still found me in his neighborhood, he was going to kill me.

I'm still alive.

I still have a voice.

I'm going to stay alive.

And keep speaking.

I promise.

Everything I wrote here has been non-fiction, but I'm too afraid to have this published as non-fiction, so I'll label it hybrid.

Except, no,

fear is hell. All of the homophobes and Islamophobes out there live in hell. Their life is hell, because fear is fire and when it expands out to the entirety of your soul, then it is eternal.

I label this as hybrid because *I* am hybrid. I'm Finn and Karelian and Greek and Saami and Balkan and French and Middle Eastern and more. I'm not gay or straight but happy to be in the confusion of what's in the middle. I'm hybrid. I embrace the hybrid.

Tame and wild.

Very wild.

Reindeer

Fuck Santa.
You tell me the worst thing that ever happened to me
was finding out I'm indigenous.
But fuck Santa.
The reindeer were the heart of our religious symbolism

up until the time they turned us into witches.
And with Christianity everything's a witch
if it isn't part of the military-industrial complexity.
"Rudolph the Red-nose Reindeer is some racist shit," Nils said
and you tell me that Nils overreacts to everything,

but there's less than 100,000 of us in the world
and you say that no one cares about the indigenous
and I can't understand why I'm dating you
and then we have sex
and I suddenly understand why,

but, seriously, when we walk into that Target,
you know the one, where you walk in and instantly
you feel like you're in Big Brother central
with cameras pointing in your face
and the metastasis of security

and the goddamn name of the place is 'Target,'
if that isn't the creepiest thing in the world
and then all the Xmas decorations
are all of these symbols and icons
of other religions

that everyone pretends are Christian,
but it's pure paganism
and Judaism
and shamanism
and all these other –isms

that Christians don't know shit about
and I'm supposed to look at this plastic reindeer
and think how cute it is
when all I can think of is the genocide of my people.
We drive home in silence.

I keep going through words in my head,
words like
Pygmy
and Kwa
and Bantu

and Munda
and Digaro
and Vedda
and Lak
and Jarawa

and Silesians

and Ni-Vanuatu
and Karelian
and Saami
and I keep thinking

What did it take to make a people unknown?
And I keep thinking
The second I get home I'm going to write about who I am.
And we get home
and I type the word "Reindeer" at the top of the page.

Death and Taxonomies

In class, I mentioned my Sámi roots and strangely
found anti-indigenous comments tarnishing bones—
America's 'melting-point' immigrant culture, how
cultures are kept under glass, under wraps, under-
ground, as if buried. & a comedian on NPR,

asked his racial makeup, said, *I don't want to*
answer that. Soon as you tell someone your
ethnicity, they start boxing you in. Boxing,
as in punches thrown. There is a cosmetology
to identity, how to cover the bruises from all

the domestic violence. My brother, who works
at a hazmat center, says he watches the raccoons
climb in and out of the biohazard bins, says he saw
a deer glowing in the dark. I ask if he's kidding
and he says there is nothing funny about America.

Pokoinikk

My best friend's father committed suicide by putting a gun in his mouth. His father was a chef with an incredibly picky taste so the sense of irony was not lost on me, but it was a revelation that I realized I could never reveal out loud.

I should add that there's nothing abnormal about dying by gun-in-mouth in the Upper Peninsula of Michigan where the gun ownership rates are huge and there's an aging population, long winters, renowned poverty, and, well, all of the ingredients for suicide.

The problem—and I suppose there were actually many problems, come to think of it—was that we were Karelian and Saami. My friend was Karelian and Saami. His father was Karelian and Saami. And I'm Karelian and Saami. Karelian and Saami and Finn. Long story short, a lot of Finns are an interweaving of the three cultures. A lot of people don't know this, but the Swedes did a genocide of forced sterilizations on the Saami who they labeled in their meticulous church files as simply "Finn." The reason was that the blonde-haired Swedes saw the indigenous skin and hair and faces and everything of the Saami and Karelians as inferior. The same attitude they had with Finns. So, naturally, Finns and Saami and Karelian intermarried. And with these three cultures, the Swedes, largely, did not intermarry. The U.P. is filled with those of Finn-Karelian-Saami descent. They estimate that there are less than a quarter million Karelians. And less than 100,000 Saami left. And when you are connected to a culture facing the possibilities of linguicide (which has already happened to several Saami languages, including Kainuu Saami, which is my background), as well as simply genocide, then suicide is looked at as a dishonor to your people. It's basically making it easier for the colonizers to exterminate a race.

My best friend owned the gun.

His name, by the way, is Nils. He says he has always been cursed ever since his parents named him after the number zero. He said his name not only means nothing, but means a plural of nothingness. Not *nil*, but Nils—an endless supply of nil. In actuality, he's named after the great Saami poet Nils-Aslak Valkeapää. He should feel honored, not horrored.

The horror comes from his guilt. Statistically, they've done studies that show that having a gun in the house minimally protects the owner, but it exponentially increases the odds of everyone else in the house being killed or injured by it. Typically, the father-owner is microscopically safer and, reciprocally, the mother (or fiancée or girlfriend or what have you) has just had an unfortunately mammoth increase in the likelihood that she'll have the lead core with steel plating that is a bullet tear through some part of her body in the near or distant future. The same is true of the children. Gun accidents kill, on average, a child everyday. And that child tends to be related to the gun's owner. Except in this instance it was the son who owned the gun. The father borrowed it.

Now I should say this, Saami and Karelians are superstitious. Very superstitious. Super-superstitious. And that word—*superstition*—is etymologically linked to *fear*. And this is what this story is about.

Nils, when he found out the news, looked like he not only just saw a ghost, but that the ghost stood directly in front of him. Inches in front of him.

I was the one who told him. Unfortunately, I poke my nose into everything. Hell, I poke each nostril and the entirety of my face into every little thing that's going on. It's my nature, the forest of my being. And that, exactly, is where Nils headed. At the words that it was his own gun that killed his father, Nils turned and walked directly outside. I was not the ghost he'd seen. It was someone else. And apparently Nils felt safer away from the prison-like walls of house. He began walking rather quickly towards the bluff where I was worried he was going to leap. The path was flattened more heavily than when we were kids, thanks to a new overpopulation in the U.P. where people much more frequently actually have neighbors, which, when I was young, was a frightening concept. Who wants someone living next door to them? That space should be dedicated to absence.

Nils stood, overlooking the city. Negaunee is a town that has been rumored to be Ojibwe for "hell." It's not true at all. (I thought that *Maji-ishkodeng* was Ojibwe for hell, but that really just translates as 'bad fire,' probably taken from old biblical translations.) Negaunee though actually means *leading*. To which some people reply, "Yeah, leading to hell." All I knew is this is the spot where Nils was led to. The city looked like a grey yawn. The clouds had the rare appearance of bulging tenth-month-of-pregnancy marshmallows. Later I'd find out they're called mammary clouds, great giant breasts in the sky. They threaten the birth of severe thunderstorms, but it was only a threat, merely harbingers.

Before I could reach my hand up to Nils' shoulder, he said, "Forty days."

I put my hand back down.

The words made no sense.

I remember a cousin of mine, after her father had drank to the point of death, the pinpoint of death, its puncturing needle. Afterwards, she said that she couldn't taste anything for weeks. I started talking about food and she said that, no, she was speaking of lips and sunlight and the air. She said that she had a severe nosebleed a few days later and it was strange how the blood in her mouth seemed to have no flavor, no viscosity, no meaning. The city seemed the same, as if its ceilings of houses and its ceiling of sky were all made of some monochromatic gruel. I looked at Nils' face and I could see the skull underneath the skin.

"Forty days is how long he'll be here."

"Who?"

"For forty days," he said. And looked at the city, as if he was wondering where to rush off to. I wanted to know why we were rushing. Death is about pausing. It's where you become a shadow, even dress like one, so that you can remain nearly immobile, collapsed to the floor with misery. But it was as if Nils refused a brush with death and instead insisted on the youthfulness of running. He climbed down the bluff, a well-worn route where the rocks were scarred from old layers of graffiti still hanging on with palimpsest incomprehensibility. I climbed down after him and then he ran, to his house, where he packed with a fury and we were suddenly in his front yard, then in his car, and he told me I should get out, but I said I wouldn't, and he said he wasn't coming back for a long time and that all I'd have was what was with me and I told him I had a wallet with a credit card and that was enough.

We drove towards Michigamme, the railroad tracks and snaking lake paralleling us to the left with its old story of a train derailment where everyone inside drowned, trapped at the bottom. There was also the boring gorgeous nature everywhere. Nils told me that the dead roam the earth for forty days. He said after those forty days, they remain silent forever. We hadn't turned on the radio once. The windows were down and I asked him if we'd drive for forty days. We stopped for the first time in northern Wisconsin, just after its river border. I wondered if we were heading south, very south. Come to find out, we headed everywhere.

For a few days, we ricocheted around camping grounds in the badger state. Every camping ground gave off summer camp splatter film series potential. I realized Nils really had the idea of running from the ghost of his father for forty days. I asked him if his father's ghost could drive too. He said no, that it would walk. Then he said it was possible it could enter a car as a passenger. He looked in the rearview mirror when he said this and then we did our longest marathon drive yet, going all the way to the mildly hill-ish and arguably hellish Bowling Green, Kentucky, without stopping for food or bathroom breaks. He handed me an empty bottle at one point and told me to climb into the backseat if I wanted privacy. I wanted to ask him what his father's ghost would do if he found him, but his reaction after his revelation that his father could hitchhike made me realize that I might possibly trigger more intense responses. My greatest fear was being left behind. We were eating nothing but diner's appetizer meals and gas station non-food for the duration of the trip so far, his own money emptying at painful speed from the gas prices alone. In Kentucky, he knew a Composition professor with missing teeth. He had a room where we could both stay. Nils told me he was glad I'd come along. He didn't want to be alone. I wondered if his father had said he would haunt his son. In the dark of the small back pseudo-bedroom I thought of Saami ghost stories, about how they are so filled with cannibalism. I decided Nils' father must be a hungry ghost. I dreamed of fangs. I wanted to know how this would end. I assumed with just the simple arrival of the fortieth day, but then after our third day in Kentucky, in the middle of night, I heard Nils whisper, "He's here." And then Nils began packing in the dark. I rushed to the bathroom, wanting to urinate without using a bottle. When I flushed, I exited to a back room that was empty. I actually opened up the bedroom window and leaped out as it seemed significantly faster that stumbling through the pitch-black house. I ran to the car and opened the door and dove in. Nils drove with the nervousness of those imprisoned. On the floor, I saw a first-aid kit, stolen. I didn't ask why. I assumed it meant there might be times where we couldn't so much as stop for a hospital.

Forty days is forever. If you don't believe me, mark it on your calendar right now and watch how long it takes.

960 hours.

57,600 minutes.

3.456 million seconds.

Imagine three million seconds when you are terrified.

I should say this though. Nils was terrified. I was not. I'd watch Nils brush his teeth like he was a wounded hare. He'd eat like he'd just emerged from a hole and was concerned of wings swooping down from overhead. He constantly used mirrors and peripheral vision. I imagined the most-killed animals of the forest, their hiding spots, how desperate they must be for relaxation. I am not terrified of anything. I don't believe in ghosts. I don't believe in my ancestors. And for that, I suppose, I can be banished forever from my Saami and Karelian community, but I am already banished from my Saami and Karelian community. I am an American, which means that we had to let go of our drums and our bear rituals and our yoik and our beliefs in order to become workers. My ancestors were reindeer herders who moon-lighted as shaman, with an emphasis on moonlight. They would go into the deep underworld for knowledge and emerge with medicine from the very dirt we stood on. Now, we are miners who step down into squamous-walled holes to emerge with the iron ore pellets that resemble musket balls, the peninsula polluted with the tiny somewhat round ammunition-like ore that seems to stain absolutely everything. I tell Nils we should go back.

He said yes, we have to.

He doesn't say why.

I assume it's because of money. I assume it's because there is nowhere for us to go. There is no hiding from ghosts, not true ghosts. We are not even halfway into the forty days. We enter Michigan in the night and there is no celebration. There even seems to be a question mark about the border. The difference between Ohio and Michigan is all sports-related. In reality, there is no difference. The states are indistinguishable. Just like this part of the night has no difference from this other part of the night that we have just entered. I look out the window, my body dead with exhaustion. I can't even move my head. I want to look forward, but I stare at the trees that seem not to be there. The woods exist, but only in the day. Dark is replaced with dark. Nils pulls over before he falls asleep driving and we wake up to a hint of morning as its soft light attempts to climb into our car. Nils is wide-awake, staring at me with his ghost-food eyes.

Nils turns and looks into the backseat. He is violently still. I want to turn and look into the backseat but I am convinced a body is there. I'm not sure if the mouth will be wide open, if the right frontal lobe will be absent, if the brainstem will be... I close my eyes and can see all of this before me, so I open my eyes immediately and look to the backseat where Nils' father hovers. He doesn't sit. He just seems to be present, impossibly, a fractured bit of self, as if we have all been like this our whole lives and not recognized how little of us there is that exists. His father does not look at me and does not look at Nils. There is no looking. It is just the hint of what was once life. I look at Nils' father's mouth but there is no mouth. It's not that it has been eradicated through violence, but rather that there was never a mouth. Just like my old philosophy teacher had proved to us, rather convincingly, that the chair he picked up and placed on top of his desk did not exist, that it never existed, that we all had accepted a shared delusion of its actuality. I started to see the car as the same and myself as the same and Nils as the same and wondered if we were being taken to hell or heaven or limbo, except for the Saami there is no heaven or hell or especially limbo; there is just the continuation of existence. A Saami reindeer herder continues to herd reindeer even in death, especially in death. Life has become a constant practice for what the infinity of death will be, the mastery of reindeer herding. A father will worry about his son and want to chase after his son and reach out to his son and ask his son what he is running from and I try to speak but cannot because it is not my father and Nils starts to speak but it is words I should not hear and so I leave the car, not in fear but in respect, and I close the door softly and stand at the side of the road watching my best friend talk to his dead father and I hear nothing but only see the emotion and there *is* emotion in the dead, not tears, but there is the feeling of want and desire and sorrow and need and time has stopped, at least stopped mattering, and I look up at what is remaining of the half of the sky that is still night with its barely made out stars that represent a celestial elk hunt, as I've been told, where even the sky is a practice of the day-to-day of living, where stars are reindeer and darkness is earth and the moon is our mother and the father is here, if for a few more days, and I fall asleep on the side of the road and when I wake up to a light that is now angry with heat, I realize that the car is gone and that I am seven hours by car from Negaunee, but by foot I am two weeks away from Negaunee and I wonder if Nils has been taken to Maji-ishkodeng. Or if I have been taken to Maji-ishkodeng. If I have been eaten by the chef father. Eaten by my revealing the horrors of his death. Eaten by my lack of belief in my people. Eaten by colonialism. Eaten by road and credit card. And I begin walking and the sun with its overpowering heat reminds me with each and every step that it is a deity and as I walk I realize that I come from a nomadic people and the fear that Nils felt was his father teaching him, haunting him, teaching him to embrace his nomad blood, his Karelian blood, his Saami blood. My blood. Blood.

The People in the Bible

weren't always in the Bible.
Before that they were in Jerusalem
and Cleveland

or wherever.
I don't know math very well,
but I know that there were twelve unsubstantiated apostles.

The twelve unsubstantiated apostles
ate a substantial meal
and it somehow got converted

into a ritual of transubstantiation,
but I'm too young to understand all this shit.
I just know that the people in the Bible

are trapped in the Bible
and Lot's wife keeps getting turned into salt
and how much does it suck to be a condiment and, worse, to be called
"Lot's Wife"

your entire life
or your entire death
or whatever,

your entirety of being salt,
mythological salt, and you can't even be as cool as mythological pepper
and you can't even have your own name

and your husband has to be called "Lot,"
which is like having a husband named A Great Deal
or A Whole Boatload of Stuff

when you just want to be married to a Jacob
or an Emily
or a Mohammed

or an Aino.
How come there's no Ainos in the Bible?
I had a great-grandpa named Aino

and 'great-grandpa' is a helluva long time ago.
My cheeks are starting to flush like a toilet thinking about all this.
I'm getting myself riled up like it's the Trump fake election again.

I can't even blink anymore without feeling like needing a drink
of red wine, blood red, with the stamp
of Jesus all over the bottle.

I went to a church yesterday, but the building had no answers for me.
It's why when the Saami worship, we go outside, into the heart and lungs
of nature
instead of being trapped in the tin cans of Christianity.

Veahkki

The head of the Native American camp pulls me aside and says that some of the kids there don't want to get their initial medical checkup.

I tell her that's fine. I ask why.

She says she doesn't want to say or shouldn't say or can't say or something.

I tell her to tell me.

She looks down at her bison burger. We are both happy because we are having bison burgers. For some reason, bison burgers just make you happy. Or maybe it's that McDonalds makes you manic-depressed. We're detoxifying as part of the Decolonizing Diet Project that's part of the camp.

She says that it's because they think I'm white.

But I'm not white, I say. Except I am white. And not white. I'm a bunch of things in a big American melting pot except I hate that term. Whenever I think of melting, it's always horrible imagery—*House of Wax* and *The Wizard of Oz* and *The Blob*. And pot makes me think of, well, pot. Great American horror movie cannabis. I don't know. The term's stupid. But I'm indigenous and not indigenous and Middle Eastern and Midwestern simultaneously and I want her to explain all of that to her campers, but instead I say that a lot of the Native Americans here get mistaken for white.

And she says, "Yes, but they're mistaking *you* for white."

And so I tell her, fine, tell them not to come. They have the right to waive their medical exam.

And she says, "But we need to know if they have anaphylactic shock risks and—all the things you said we have to worry about."

And I nod yes. And I don't even finish my burger.

I go to the lake and I listen to the loons and an Anishinaabe elder walks up and we start talking and he tells me that the outside world will drive you insane because the outside world is an inside world. He says it's a cubicle world out there and a prison world and a closet world and he said when you come out of the cubicle and out of the prison and out of the closet, you should go immediately to the woods and the lake because that's where the sanity is. I ask him about medicine and he tells me that the ground is filled with medicine. He says that we're standing on medicine right now and he points to a Cattail and asks what those are good for and I say, "I don't know, everything" and he laughs and says, yes, but he says that they are extraordinary in soup. And I ask what kind of soup and he says, "Cattail soup. Or you add it to other soups. That's my favorite food in the world."

"What?"

"Cattails. Ever since I was a boy."

I ask him if it's a mistake to be doing medicine, if I should get out of the medical field. And he asks what sort of things I've done as a medic and I tell him, "I don't know, CPR."

And he says, "And CPR isn't indigenous?"

"Is it?"

"There are stories of Cherokee tying those who were in cardiac arrest to horses and then having the horses gallop at a speed where the body would bounce up and down so that it was just like the compressions of CPR."

"No way."

"You know 'syringes'?"

"Of course."

"South American indigenous healers."

"What?"

"First to use them."

The loons in the lake spoke to us. We listened to a follow-up moment of silence.

"I could give you a long list," he said and walked away. He was making a birchbark canoe by hand, every single element of it homemade, including the tools. I watched its white cedar ribs.

I went back to the nursing station. A group of students were lined up. I saw the holes of those who were missing. I had to focus on who was present. I actually had to work on my mind to do that, reminding myself of this moment, this second, these people's needs, our needs, who was here. I was. The ancestors were. They were around us at all times.

I set up my stethoscope, sphygmomanometer, pulse ox, and other equipment. As the students came up to me one at a time, I imagined them as reindeer, as bear, trying to treat their arms gently, as holy, realizing these are people who have survived genocide. I let the indigenous part of my blood and body control every movement, every action, promising for the next few hours I would be completely Sámi, utterly aboriginal. Listening on my stethoscope, I could hear their pulses and breath blending with the voices of the loons.

For the People Who are Indigenous

"the rigors of an Arctic sky"
—Bamewawagezhikaquay

I'm tied forever to history.
We're extinct like the footsteps
on the hardwood floor.

For my people, there are a hundred
words for *snow*, for *reindeer*.
In Islam there are a hundred words

for *camel*, for *know*.
My counselor last Thursday told me
that families with genocide

in their roots tend to pass down
the ability for muscled silence;
there are entire cities repressed in soot

and smoke. I'm sick, wishing
for a knife to slice my guts
open, pull out the forced sterilization,

the way that our bear rituals
turned into McDonald's,
shifted our drum circles

into FM radio repetition.
I have a moon in my chest.
It is on fire.

This is the First Poem You Have Bled By Someone of Saami Descent

When you escape genocide, there is no promise of jobs—
the forced sterilization of Swedish eugenics, my grandparents
hid in the northest north of Michigan, where the indigenous shake
drums, jingle-dress bliss, full of Bamewawagezhikaquay maps.
I have bear ritual in my veins, in the rowboats of my head.

I need aurora borealis to live, to revert to Sápmi kayaks
while I struggle for food in this post-Obama mood where
the leaders haven't stepped inside of schools, let alone
inside pow wows, where Detroit is not allowed, where pan-
sexual affinities are proud despite the laws that low the crowd.

My Indigenous Roots
Have Been Buried

for April Lindala, Sally Brunk
Lone Caribou, Bamewawagezhikaquay
& Gordon Henry

Margaret Noodin says the ghosts come for bones.
In Sámi, *jápmin* comes for the *dákti*. Bones
are *hard seed*. We grow once we are buried,
not erased, as long as you will allow being buried
to mean that you embrace being raised as a tree.
You honeymoon with the sky. My family tree
is buried. I am digging it up. In Sámi, "to be
on the brink of death" is one word—*jápmigoahtit*.
Goahtit—to start to do something. To start death.
We begin to tower into the collaboration of death.
We go at it like night kicking sun. *Goahtit*—
we all need to "start to do something." Or we'll be
lost to the ghosts hungry for the world's bones.

I Am

for Kayla Bell,
Johan Turi,
& Elmer Riekki

i: *okta*

aboriginal. And my father says
that I have a polar bear for a mother,
a beluga father, that he is proud
to be Kainuu, Kuusamo, an inability
to trace the Saami roots, the Karelian
connections, so far, but I keep digging,
not like the grave invaders of Minnesota,
but like someone searching for home.

ii: *guokte*

"No one can own a lake." I am
growing up in a county owned by meth.

   Consider failing.
A dead man must be alone, whether he wants it

or not. You can watch the blood slowly succumbing
to gravity, the way that losing means down, how
lightning likes to tear open anything reaching

for sky.

iii: *golbma*

"No one can own the sky." I am
asking the Scandinavian Studies Professor
if I can take his class.

He tells me Saami
aren't Scandinavians,
says, *What would you even
write about?* My ancestors
come from the heart
of the *Kalevala*; I tell him
I'd like to write about
the importance of having
a literature. He tells me
that the *Kalevala* is stolen
from Sweden. He says
I would have to write
about that. I've never
heard this. He seems
like a dream of snakes,
a dream-life cliff
where serpents wait
at the edge. I want
to tell him I think in Saami,
but I don't have the confidence,

remain silent, like the thousands
and thousands of Saami
that Sweden forced into sterilization,
trying to make a race extinct.
Sometimes I think about that empty
seat in the classroom.

iv: *njeallje*

"No one can own me." I am
craving living this life over, so that
I could be more peaceful, less jumbled.

I would also sleep less.
And thank my parents
repeatedly, like a consecration.
I'd work in a homeless shelter.
No, not work. I'd *joy* in a home-
less shelter. I'd encourage you
to go to the homeless shelter,
to bathe in talk, to eat beans
and listen, to gut life, to kiss,
to kiss strangers, to kiss
librarians, to kiss so often
that you can feel cheeks
on your lips even here,
even now, without anyone
on your skin. Run.
Hell, I'd even kiss Death.

v: *vihtta*

                                    I am
searching and researching and re-searching
my genealogy, finding a burial certificate
where a great-great-grandfather's cause
of death was marked as: *Drunk.*
I find the ship they came on—the Mauretania—
that it was exactly a hundred years ago,
my grandfather born one year
before Sweden's ethnic cleansing
of us, an attempt to end continuation.
I think of the family trees in our backyard
in Suomi, how I'd walk to school
in ways that no map would register,
embracing bluffs and getting lipstick
all over the clouds.

I'm Sámi

Disgruntled indigenous. So cool that I'm Arctic. A heart like
an icepick. I'm sorry, but I'm not white. I'm not right in your eyes,
the color of my skin a shade off, a shadow often hid in the blizzard
wind. You'll find me north. Further north. So north that I'm south.
You're snow-blind. I walk home, straight, while you walk backwards.
I'm born in the backwoods, Eskimo-blooded. You can intuit that
I'm Inuit-offshoot, Michigan reincarnated, but more fjord than
Ford. Sauna-lunged. Alcohol-raped. Worked in a mine that isn't
mine. Waterlogged. A government wind farm forced on our land,
reindeer-land, reigned over, resigned, reformed in a new north,
where the poverty isn't poetry. We are *sisu*. It means persistence. We
are. Like *hullu*, we are. Through hell and high snow, we are.

Vuorwro

At an Anishinaabe summer camp recently, I asked an Abenaki elder what this region's ideas were on ghost stories. Could they be told? Should they be told? We were on a lake kayaking at the time and he told me to shut my eyes and listen.

"Open them."

I did.

He asked me what I heard.

I told him a robin, a loon, several ducks, the wind, a fish.

"What type of fish?"

I didn't know.

He told me the ancestors know. He told me they could hear a fish a mile away. He told me they would hear my ghost stories and he asked me what ghost stories are.

I didn't know how to describe them.

"What is the difference between an ancestor and your 'ghost'?"

I said, "In Saami tradition, we tell ghost stories."

He told me to tell ghost stories then with the Saami, but he said with the Anishinaabe you should do as the Anishinaabe do. He said every action will be seen and then he paddled into the wind with ease.

I struggled to catch up with him.

There was a fire that night with jingle dresses and drums. There was a moment later, after the fire was nearly out, where there were only three of us left. Then two. The one person left was a white man. A boy. A twenty-year-old. He said he heard that I like to tell stories.

I asked him if he saw what was in the bushes earlier. I told him it was there now. A man with a knife. I enjoyed seeing the moon of fear in his young eyes.

But then, very shortly after I said this, an elder stepped out of the bushes, frowning.

I became silent. The fire went out. We sat in the darkness. I bowed my head and walked away and when I did I could hear his cracking voice say, "We should never be afraid of the woods."

I disappeared into the shadows.

I thought about that 'we.' The twenty-year-old was white, but he had expressed how he only felt like he fit in with the indigenous. I was indigenous, but I had blended in too deeply with the whites.

Several nights later, after the camp had ended, while watching a James Wan horror movie, I heard my roommate say to me from his bedroom, "You should be watching *Sami Blood*, not *Saw*." *Saami Blood* is an Amanda Kernell film about prejudice against the Saami.

By the way, I suddenly realized that this—*what I am writing right now*—might be the only thing you have ever read by a person of Saami descent.

I have been suicidal and resisted it based solely upon my anger at the possibilities of extinction. How could I kill myself when there are so few Saami in the world? Instead I remain alive with a fury. You must be alive to tell stories. Unless you write them down. But you must remain alive in order to write down as many stories as possible. Including ghost stories.

But I do worry about the ghost story... although the reality is that our folklore is filled with ghosts, jam-packed with ghosts and trolls and trickster spirits and the sky is one gigantic celestial elk hunt. We see the snowflakes as the galloping of reindeer. My ancestors are reindeer herders and I tend to herd stories, to gather them, and feed them, and love them. Even when they are laced with fear.

I am telling you all of this to explain Vuorwro to you.

Vuorwro:

She will come into your room at night and eat you.

There is a lot of eating of human flesh in Saami folklore.

But I shouldn't use that term. I spoke with an elder while climbing Sugarloaf Mountain and he was very displeased with that word. I never used it again around him, but white omnipresence keeps bringing that word back into my usage.

Vuorwro is real and folklore and authentic and metaphor and literal and more all at the same time. I know an elder said bears raised her and that she can make tornadoes the way that other women can make soup, and I believe her. I do not take it as metaphor. I take it as fact. I believe her.

And with Vuorwro—I did not know this until much later—she can only enter into bedrooms that have no water. This is true.

And this is also true:

When I first started dating my long-time girlfriend, I came to find that she suffers from both narcolepsy and polydipsia (or excessive thirst). She keeps multiple water bottles filled throughout the apartment. She sleeps next to water. She will have cups and bottles and little mugs with third-filled water and to-the-rim-filled water and chamomile and passionflower and valerian teas. Teas for thirst and for sleep. I can't get up in the night without kicking a glass. At first, it drove me mad. And then, later, I learned that she has kept Vuorwro from our bedroom for years.

She is not Saami either, my girlfriend. Not aboriginal at all. I talked with my Abenaki friend recently and he said he would never date someone who wasn't native. He said native women are inherently strong and wise and faithful. But he said that if he did end up with someone who's not indigenous, it would mean that the ancestors had a plan for him he did not see.

For me, I have my water-protector. My woman of sleep and safety.

And I am going to cuddle into her thirsty arms now, safe from Vuorwro.

To the Seven Bars in Our Town of 4,614 People

There are so many wars. The wars of now. The wars of control. The wars of Dantean fourth circles of Hell. Toivo walks out. He chambers out. He tumbles out onto the prose street. He vomits babies. We watch. Shakespeare plummets out of his mouth. All of the deaths at the end. We go home. Storm clouds are coming. They look like America.

The Rejection of the Upper Peninsula of Michigan

for Martti Ahtisaari
& Arne Kauppinen

The Bible says that your hometown will turn you to night.
Or perhaps it's that where you were born descends your heart?
Or maybe the translation should be: there are no mothers left

in hometowns, that there is only evacuation? My ancestors
were refugees. I have diaspora in my arteries. Karelian and Balkan
and Saami and genocide and *tvångssteriliseringar*—the word

is like a disease—in my background, on my back, the weight
on my shoulders. I worry about extinction. I have panic attacks
about extinction. I swallow my tongue in the early morning

because of the threat of extinction. We went from the attic
of Finland to the attic of Michigan to a place where unemployment
is the sunset... Or is it that no prophet is acceptable anywhere?

My Indigenous Roots

in my family tree
have been cut down
by the logging company.
I actually found
a piece of land
that doesn't look
painted by muck
and death and
the birds in my
branches are being
strangled by sky.

Is that God peeing
acid rain? Only white
in this white-making
country, its painting
over everything, night
becomes day, Native
soul and heart becomes
Caucasian, when I'm from
a place no whites live.
I'm mix and mix
means I don't exist.

I Grew Up in a Town So Cold That Even the Ice Could Not Commit Suicide

We would walk home backwards, even in summer,
just to keep up the practice. Our house would be buried
in white, the world cocained, and we'd punch each other
at bus stops for heat. This was in a north so north
that there was more reindeer than rain. I love-hated the attic
of the Arctic, my Saami-Finn youth, my lichen life,
the way we were almost extinct, almost invisible
in the aurora borealis perfection, as if the sky was dancing
to Armageddon, the winter lasting forever, the Witch
owning everything. My grandfather was a shaman.
He told me to fear heat. I remember his theater eyes.

Indigenous

I am proud
that I am indigenous
even if I am
European indigenous,
the confusion
of explaining
that there are Native Europeans—
Saami, Komi, Yupik, Karelian—
and when someone says
Eskimo, I want to stab them
in their knives.
The intense beauty of being
around your people—the intense
anger that they are critically
endangered, that the language
is dying, breathless,
aporic, wishing to exist
with the intensity
of death.

Saami-American

That hyphen, signaling separation,
the segregation of history, how we
came to the U.S. to escape the hollow
pits of eugenics, the way the U.P.
seemed so similarly Arctic, the bear
rituals left behind, our drums left
behind, our lectures in the new land
of Armageddon and how we had to
give our heart to Jesus or we would
burn in a hell so far from the ice
of our backstory, the aurora borealis
of earthquake-sunshine and nothing
makes sense now, especially the mines
that took and took and take with
the noon shaking of the city when
the dynamite owns everything
and it makes me think of Atja,
the god of lightning if she'd been
bottled and forced into slavery.

Setting the Landlord on Fire

Let me explain something first.
This was by mistake.
Although I remember a motivational speaker
saying something about how there are no mistakes.
And it was only his face.
I was trying to do a circus trick.
I was drunk.
He had a giraffe shirt on
so I couldn't miss him.
I spit the vodka aflame into his face

and he had a beard
and mustache—*had*—
and fell back
into the Christmas tree,
which wasn't my Christmas tree,
because I'm not Christian
and I don't own a saw.
I'm Saami,
which is a silenced
people

so maybe this is the first time you've ever heard of us,
in this poem
about my landlord
rolling around
in the thorns
or whatever
of silver and gold
classic-meets-mod
orbs and beads and crucifixes
that unfortunately

do stick in backs
and he didn't die
or even get wounded
that badly.
It was more embarrassment.
Like every time I go to the slot
and put the check in
and realize I can't even hear it
hit the bottom.
I don't even have the satisfaction of that.

"Kiálláseh" by Amoc, featuring Ailu Valle

I'm proud of my Sámi roots. And part of that pride is the ability to survive the threat of extinction that hovers over so many indigenous groups. I was reading recently that Sámi, Ojibwe, and Inuit cultures look like they will have longevity due to their cultural strength. Amoc's "Kiálláseh" featuring Ailu Valle is part of that Sámi muscle. There is a pulsing beauty to the Sámi language and it's heard in the rhythms of Amoc's *"psykedelij"* lyrics of áárvuh and *jaska* and *siälu piälust*, words that flash across the screen in the video in large letters that help to further shout out the need for continuance, of linguistic existence. Hip-hop has frequently addressed genocide and survival and Amoc is its leading voice for the Saamelaiset. Each time I hear it, I feel the *nuórahtu* in my bones, the north wind, my Arctic heart that assimilation tries to drown.

My Ancestors

My grandmother's grandmother hid,
buried herself under handfuls of history,

and now I am discovering—through the thaw
of genocide—the glaciers of bravery

in my Arctic blood, my Jewish blood,
my Muslim blood, our multiracial story.

Shaman / *Noaidi*

I'm a star	*dasste*
sometimes,	*idja*
	idja
good	*idja*
	idja
at blinking	*idja*
in the night.	*idja*

The *Novealla* of Vuorwro (#6)

for Weldon Kees,
Nils-Aslak Valkeapää,
and Erik Blomberg's Aslak

I've never read a poem
about the throats of ghosts,
but my Sámi blood aches
to tell you, no, warn you,
of the thick thirst the dead
have for our hintings of breath,

the way that we seem so dead
yet alive in our sleep, a perfect
balance between this world
and the next, and I imagine
Vuorwro standing, no, floating
above us in our sleep, admiring

our necks, hearing the theater
of our hearts, sensing the heat
of our skin, and then realizing

that she can bathe in our blood
faster than we can wake.
Vuorwro can only eat souls

of those who have no water
in their rooms; this is the myth,
no, the story, the story told

as true in my youth, of her mouth,
the way it can open, tongue out,
the voice of her teeth speaking,

the sound of her slaughter, a sickness
of doom, the tingling of her night-

wandering, as she goes from room
to room, her avant-garde hair

a tangle of angry language, and
a final warning from my mother,

that if you have a cup of water
and feel safe, never look out

your window at the sky, caught
up in what you might think

is a reindeer floating across
the starred black, only to have

her shift form, the window open

like a mouth and suddenly your

soul is sucked, like from a straw,

and you are pulled into Hell.

This was our bedtime story,

no, myth, no, warning of the war

between the corporeal and the non-,
how we should be aware
of being fish-hooked by blood,
turned to blood, cooked in blood,
if we do not keep our blood
true as the iciest north winds.

Collusion

I walked into the hospital and the nurse said, "Get her out of here before she dies on me."

It destroys hospital statistics when patients die.

The nurse could argue that she wanted the patient to be around family and not E.R. ruins.

When I transport patients to the hospitals, hospices, homes, I look out the ambulance windows. When the patients are stable, I glance at the road, the side of the road, the woods that fill with night, become soaked in moon, and I see absence.

A Tallahassee judge recently ruled Florida black bear hunting as legal.

How many black bears are in Delaware, Hawaii, Illinois, Indiana, Iowa, Kansas, Nebraska, North Dakota, and South Dakota combined?

Susan Mitchell's poem "The Bear" opens with a bear dancing and then it becomes an image of a bear, lost to memory.

There are no black bears in those nine states.

Ten black bears in all of Rhode Island.

Fifty in Alabama, according to blackbearsociety.org.

When I go to work, I pass by a gun store that changes quotes on its sign every week, saying things like, "It's Father's Day, buy him a rifle" or "All we are saying is give guns a chance."

When patients seem like they're dying, you can feel a sense of controlled panic coming from the EMTs. You can feel a hint of brilliant fear in their voice when they yell up to me that the blood pressure keeps rising, or falling.

The worry is when numbers suddenly change. You don't want patients who are hypo- or hyper-. You don't want brady- or tachy-. You want homeostasis, that perfect state of *homoios* and *stasis*. A word that came into being in 1926—just before the rice rat became extinct, just after the Kenai Peninsula wolf became extinct, just before the heath hen became extinct, just after the California grizzly bear became extinct.

Became.

From the Old English *becuman*, 'to be or do something.'

The jarring of 'to be' with 'extinct.'

I remember a patient looking up past me, through the ceiling, up into the neck of God, deep into the accidents of angels, the way that their wings batter together to crack open death.

I wonder sometimes if all of the unseen hypothetical bears could be turned into one patient in the back of an ambulance, a solitary bear with ventricular fibrillation, a bear with a ballistic trauma, a sucking chest wound, how there might not be apathy then, how the natural inclination is always to stop bleeding, to continue breathing, to keep life.

In the military, when I was in 30 Foxtrot, a petty officer made me go around the building killing birds. I did my best to fake their deaths. I pretended to smash eggs, heads, but he watched me, insisting I kill. I went to a pastor on base and he asked if I was a consciousness objector. I told him that so much killing is done for sport, to cure boredom, to earn medals, to turn hate to smoke, to fight dead fathers, to please those who actually find no pleasure in death. I told him none of this. I simply said I wasn't. I was afraid not to be. I was cryptology. I helped transmit messages of coordinates for death. I was young. After, I had survivor's guilt. I had PTSD. I had to go to China, to get away from America. I did. I remember looking inside an ambulance in Shanghai and being amazed at how filled it was with nothing. Simply a bench inside. Traditional Chinese medicine doesn't allow for the extravagance of bag-valve masks and flashlights and nasopharyngeal airways that clutter American ambulances. They say that if a crash happens, the person most likely to get killed isn't the patient, but the paramedic in back;

they'll be hit by so much flying debris—oxygen tanks and AEDs and life-packs—that they'll have multiple injuries. Accidents on top of accidents. It'd be like being drowned by acid rain and water pollution and climate change all at the same time. It would be like being hunted by semi-automatic rifles that shoot over a hundred rounds a minute, which is what the terrorist group known as the NRA supports.

I once transported a gunshot victim who had severe diarrhea. It was the fastest I've ever seen my partner drive. He was panicked with worry simply because he didn't want to deal with the smell.

What are the five senses of extinction?

What is the odor of vanishing?

Sometimes, when I have a stable patient and I know they're doing well, I'll look out the window for a few seconds and see marsh that seems so filled with sky, as if heaven has collapsed onto earth, as if happiness lies in the breath of water and I wonder when we'll wake up, when we'll breathe the air of the divine, instead of all of this wind that is so filled with collision.

On the Road in Colorado

on the back of his Harley
I hung onto my uncle
who was barely hanging on
to life, and I'd just talked
with his daughter in Orem
who was barely hanging on
to her job, and I could feel
the tribe in me barely able
to survive in an America
where we were planning
to entrap the moon in a net
so that we could sell it
for money for bombs
that we would then sell
for thick cigarettes to smoke
to choke all the children
until they too surrendered
to the success of selling
the red hats of hatred.

I Am the Only Saami

in the middle of Lake Mohave with the Anishinaabe
who is shirtless with no life jacket and so I take

mine off too, but leave my shirt on, and we're not
really in the middle of the lake; it's much more like

two-thirds of the lake, away from where we
hear the chants that ache us to come back, but

we are here to talk, or no, we're here to listen, to the ice
in the wind and then he tells me he's not at

all Anishinaabe, but Abenaki, Algonquian, lost
from his people, but found, now, in these people.

My Girlfriend and Her Two Friends, A Mile Outside Yosemite

My girlfriend comes home from Yosemite,
says driving there, for the first time in her life,

she saw a bear. She said it crossed the road like
a monk, as if it was Thich Nhát Hanh, looking twice

at the car with soft keyhole eyes, and its body as wide
as the stars. She said she cried for the final mile of their drive.

i have been warned not to write about this (the erasure of moon so there is only sun)

the deer
at the hazmat site
where i work
eat radioactive leaves
& the raccoons wobble
by the inhalation hazard sign
and there are no birds

Saami (ruovttugiella[1])

When I write about being Saami, my sister
cringes. She doesn't want us to be indigenous,
but rather middle-class. My father is divorced
from his heritage, the nuns having beaten
my grandfather's fingers if he ever spoke
a word of a language that is now dead.
And I think of the death of language, how
the heart of words stops hyper-perfusing
so that the hands grow cold and the letters
turn pale and the lungs cease. I want to be
indigenous, but it is more than writing poems.
It's becoming a shadow to drums, covering
yourself in the stillness of your ancestors.

---

1   The language spoken at home.

The White Kid at the Native American Camp

explains indigeneity to the indigenous.
This is at the bonfire where he starts to tell a ghost story
not realizing that there are ancestors next to all of us
listening
and to create fear of the woods
is to create fear of sanity
and the boy talks on and on
as we sit silently
waiting
to see if he will listen
to the trees
that speak
when you are wise enough
to be still.

Same

I'm Saami. Or Same. Or Sami. Or Sámi. I'm going to tell you every-thing I know about my culture. It will be flash non-fiction. That's the prob-lem with being part of a culture that flirts with extinction, that fondles extinction, fucks extinction, is that your history feels written by an eraser. As if your history is melting. It is.

I don't speak Saami.

Kainuu Saami, the language where my ancestors come from, is now extinct. A dead language. I think of corpse words. A letter *s* rotting. The stench of the *č*. The rigor mortis of *l*'s.

An Anishinaabe teacher (Miskwaaopwaaganikewe Lancaster) told me that it is necessary for me to say *giitu*, Saami for 'thank you.' I need to keep the word alive, she said. She doesn't say 'thank you' in English. She says *Miigwech*. She has told me *miigwech* multiple, multiple times. She has put *miigwech* into my body. I can feel the *miigwech*. (*Giitu* for that.)

I want my culture to survive, but I don't know enough.

I know about Vuorwro, the demon-ghost of Saami culture that goes from room to room in the night looking for people who do not have any water nearby. She eats those people. She swallows their mouth and salivary glands and eats their pharynx and esophagus and everything and stomach and small intestine and medium intestine and large intestine and extra-large intestine and digests their rectum and their accessory glands, but not their ancestor glands. No one can take your ancestor glands.

She's always hungry. She's never thirsty.

I'm hungry for my culture, my actual culture.

Karelia is a clothing brand.

Riekkis is a fly-fishing brand.

I want actual Karelia. Actual Riekkis in my life.

In Saami, north means near the water. It means where the water is. It doesn't mean our north. Or your north. Or their north.

I'm Arctic. I'm attic. I'm art. I'm an addict. I come from a family of addicts. They are addicted to alcohol and bowling and heroin and horseshoes and methadone and trivia and drawing and pornography and capitalism and hope and a lot of times they die young.

My Saami grandmother drank herself to death in her twenties. My father found her dead on the floor and tucked her in. He didn't know she was dead. He was young, very young. He didn't know.

I read Sherman Alexie a lot. He talks about alcohol the ax of alcohol the rot of alcohol the anti-drum of alcohol the alcohol of alcohol. Alcohol's a rapist.

Sweden did compulsory sterilizations of the Saami. For decades. The 1940s, 1950s, 1960s, 70s. This isn't eons ago. This is yesterday.

I'll repeat it: Sweden did forced sterilizations of the Saami.

My father has found peace in saunas. He escapes into saunas whenever he can. We used to have one in the house, but he moved to Florida where the state is a sauna.

I am Karelian too. Indigenous Karelian.

Said to me once during a job interview: *You're too white to be indigenous.* I wanted to say, "You're too racist to be a job interviewer."

I wanted to say that one of my happiest moments was at a recent Native American camp, but to be more exact about the happiest I've ever been was when I was out on the lake at that Native American camp. Way out on the lake. Especially when we found a second lake, one with warning signs telling us we were trespassing. It felt good to trespass.

The Saami believe the ghosts of dead children can be found out in the tundra. You can see them if you look deep out of your window at night into the blizzard. They are standing there, looking at you, for warmth.

An Abenaki who was arrested at Standing Rock and actually put in a dog kennel for storage—if that doesn't speak volumes about the police and the indigenous—told me he would only marry an indigenous woman. He said only indigenous women have enough strength and power and honesty and beauty. He's in his forties, single. I hope he finds his indigenous cloud and wind and heart and kissing.

Her-it-age

for Jan Kauppinen
and Iriea Hokkanen

I have ice
in my arteries.
I imagine
icicle veins
where my bones

are white-yellow
like pissed-on
snow, & my father
has told me a thousand
times of my Arctic heart,

how it is melting & how *we*
are as endangered as wood bison
& Eskimo curlew, how the tundra
has been turned into the 2018 Toyota Tundra
& the Saami name has been usurped by something as evil as the

'Sporting Arms and Ammunition Manufacturers' Institute' with its sick
hacktongue hate that reminds me of the painful opening of the 1937
film *A Star is Born*,

the unnecessary Techniracist rant against Indians, and I want to yell that
I have a voice
in my arteries

  I imagine
  icicle megaphones
  where my bones
  are heard
  and not pissed on

by the *now*, & my father & mother
aren't strangled by a thousand
years of history, its heartless heart,
how we are melting & how we
are melting & how we are melting

  & how we are

About the Author

Ron Riekki is a Saami-American, Karelian-American, and Finnish-American author of fiction, non-fiction, and poetry. Riekki's books include *U.P.: a novel* and *Posttraumatic: A Memoir*. Riekki also edited *Undocumented: Great Lakes Poets Laureate on Social Justice*, *The Many Lives of The Evil Dead: Essays on the Cult Film Franchise*, *And Here: 100 Years of Upper Peninsula Writing, 1917-2017*, *Here: Women Writing on Michigan's Upper Peninsula* (Independent Publisher Book Award), and *The Way North: Collected Upper Peninsula New Works* (awarded as a Michigan Notable Book by the Library of Michigan). Riekki's poetry has been published in *Spillway*; *Poetry Northwest*; *Rattle*; *Tar River*; *Dunes Review*; *River Teeth*; *I-70 Review*; *Tipton Poetry Journal*; *Hotel Amerika*; *Little Patuxent Review*; *The New Verse News*; *Verse Wisconsin*; *Beloit Poetry Journal*; *Mizna: Film, Literature, and Art Exploring Arab America*; and many other literary journals. His fiction has been published in *The Threepenny Review*, *Bellevue Literary Review*, *Wigleaf*, *Prairie Schooner*, *Akashic Books*, *Juked*, *New Ohio Review*, *Cleaver*, *Puerto del Sol*, and many other literary journals. Riekki's story "Accidents" received the 2016 Shenandoah Fiction Prize and "The Family Jewel" was selected for *The Best Small Fictions 2015*.

Apprentice
House Press
Loyola University Maryland

Apprentice House is the country's only campus-based, student-staffed book publishing company. Directed by professors and industry professionals, it is a nonprofit activity of the Communication Department at Loyola University Maryland.

Using state-of-the-art technology and an experiential learning model of education, Apprentice House publishes books in untraditional ways. This dual responsibility as publishers and educators creates an unprecedented collaborative environment among faculty and students, while teaching tomorrow's editors, designers, and marketers.

Outside of class, progress on book projects is carried forth by the AH Book Publishing Club, a co-curricular campus organization supported by Loyola University Maryland's Office of Student Activities.

Eclectic and provocative, Apprentice House titles intend to entertain as well as spark dialogue on a variety of topics. Financial contributions to sustain the press's work are welcomed. Contributions are tax deductible to the fullest extent allowed by the IRS.

To learn more about Apprentice House books or to obtain submission guidelines, please visit www.apprenticehouse.com.

Apprentice House
Communication Department
Loyola University Maryland
4501 N. Charles Street
Baltimore, MD 21210
Ph: 410-617-5265 • Fax: 410-617-2198
info@apprenticehouse.com • www.apprenticehouse.com

CPSIA information can be obtained
at www.ICGtesting.com
Printed in the USA
LVHW081617241019
635238LV00012B/1138/P